YOUR CAREER AS A
FASHION DESIGNER

A CAREER AS A FASHION DESIGNER begins in your imagination. Are you a person who looks at clothing, shoes and hats as they pass by and imagine another way that they might have been made to look, a different color, perhaps, or another fabric choice, or a change in emphasis of some feature? Do you look at the world around you and see the pattern of shadows a fence casts on a wall and picture a coat with that same pattern? Do you notice the color of the sky on a late afternoon in summer just as storm clouds move to cover the sun and think what an elegant shade that would be for a shirt? Do you feel how comfortable to the touch is the wood used in the benches at a railway station? Imagine how excellent it would be to have buttons made with the same kind of wood? If these are typical of the types of thoughts that go through your mind, then you are on the right track when it comes to considering a career as a fashion designer.

This is not an easy career by any means. It is a highly competitive category with many ego-driven participants, some with dreams of glory that may make them less than pleasant to be around, much less work with. Nevertheless, there are many kind, creative, and cooperative people in the industry, which is a good thing since so much of what goes into the development and marketing of new fashion designs is a team effort.

If you know you were born to be a fashion designer then you should consider getting the best training you can find so that the gifts you have can be developed to their fullest. Of course, it is possible to have a career as a fashion designer without a formal education, but there is much to be learned in a college or technical school program, including how to prepare a portfolio, the necessary steps to landing a job or, if you are determined to be your own boss, to win the confidence of potential clients.

In fact, one of the earliest decisions you will likely make as a would-be fashion designer is whether you are going to seek employment with a manufacturer, or whether you plan to go out on your own. About a third of all fashion designers are self-employed, meaning they have their own shops or companies where they sell their own designs, and perhaps some creations of friends and colleagues. These independent fashion designers can also work on a contract basis for apparel manufacturers.

It is possible that until your career takes off, you will have to do other work to support yourself while moving toward your goals. Within the fashion industry there are opportunities to work with established designers as an intern or an assistant. If you have the skills, you can work as a fashion illustrator or in construction, sewing garments, or in the business end of fashion design, helping to set up displays and shows. Whatever you can do to get your foot in the door is worthwhile in this competitive field.

THINGS TO DO NOW

THERE ARE MANY THINGS YOU CAN do now to prepare for your career as a fashion designer. You need to think about the classes you should be taking. These should include anything related to art, especially practical training like drawing, painting, sculpture, and computer design. Classes in art appreciation and art history should also be on your schedule. Take business classes, as well. You may eventually start your own design business or open a retail boutique.

You should participate in your school's theater program, volunteering to work on the costume crew for student shows. This can give you great hands-on experience in sewing, becoming familiar with fabrics, handling fittings – all aspects of the work you will do if you start your career with a clothing manufacturer, and if you go out on your own. Find a local community theater group or local college where they present plays, or even a regional theater. There is always a demand for backstage help and volunteers are greatly appreciated.

for students who want to be artists, or they may be organizations for art lovers who take trips together to museums and galleries. It is imperative for anyone interested in fashion design to visit art museums, where the clothing throughout the centuries is on display. Also, visit history and natural history museums, where you can see authentic costumes and historically accurate period costume reproductions, as well as painted representations.

You should spend time in boutiques in your area to see what other designers are up to. Go to fashion shows if there are any where you live. Check listings of charity events, because fashion shows are often put on to raise funds for nonprofit organizations. If there are such events, volunteer to help out. If there are showrooms in your city, see if there are opportunities to work as an intern or after school, or if there are summer jobs available. Get to know the designers working there and see if one of them is willing to mentor you. Designers are usually overworked and happy to have an extra pair of hands.

You will want to read as many fashion magazines as possible. There are many available, displaying everything from the high end to what is happening on the fringes of the industry. Don't just stick to new editions. Go to your library and see if they have any older magazines archived, where you can look at fashion from the recent past and even trace the evolution of fashion over previous decades.

Start making clothes yourself. There is no reason to wait if you have the desire and can create a workspace and get the materials you need. If you have been working with a theater group at your school or elsewhere, you might be able to borrow its costume space when it is not being used for a show.

HISTORY OF THE FASHION DESIGN PROFESSION

IT IS PROBABLE THAT SOME EARLY human ancestor decided to alter his or her bodily covering of animal skins or plant-based materials to make it look more attractive than the outfit being worn by the person living one cave over. It is not unreasonable for us to think of that cave dweller as the first fashion designer. It is fair to assume that individual members of primitive hunting and gathering societies continued to decorate and modify the clothing they wore. These peoples tended to be mobile and needed to travel light. It would have been sensible that valuable possessions would be worn on the body – like necklaces, headgear, or furs.

No true fashion design emerged until humans began to settle in cities. As these first communities developed, and trade among them became an important aspect of civilization, new opportunities were created for professions related to all forms of art and decoration, including fashion design. While it is generally thought that cloth was home spun and woven, the dying of cloth was handled by specialists.

Dyed cloth was most likely created for the wealthy ruling classes of these civilizations, who were also served by professional artists who decorated their palaces and created jewelry out of precious stones and metals. We can imagine individuals among the nobility figuring ways to drape their clothing and place accessories to maximize attractiveness. As new clothing materials were introduced, such as wool and silk, the development of professional fashion design for the upper classes continued to evolve.

In the Byzantine Empire and in China, fabric manufacturing became concentrated into larger operations that served the courts and upper classes. Designers created patterns and images for the fabrics, and a line can be traced from these anonymous in-house designers, to the ones working in-house for clothing manufacturers today.

From the ancient world through the fall of Rome and into the Dark Ages, little is known about whether fashion design was treated as a separate profession, or if some combination of cloth manufacturers, jewelers, and servants or slaves with imagination and taste, were counted on to provide fashion advice to the nobility of the day. Commoners, we can presume, were on their own to provide simple and utilitarian garments.

Historians generally agree that fashion, as we think of it today, begins about the middle of the 1300s, as the Crusades renewed contact between Europe and Asia bringing fabrics and dyes from the East. Beginning with the Renaissance, fashion design for the upper classes set the standards for apparel for the emerging middle classes. There were some common design elements throughout the courts of Europe, but many individual styles appeared in different countries.

One of the most notable changes was the rapid turnover in styles, something unprecedented. Prior to this period, clothing styles would be unchanged for centuries at a time.

The beginning of the 20th century saw the rise of *haute couture* or high fashion, and the emergence of fashion designers as celebrities such as Dior, Chanel and Schiaparelli. These designers dressed the upper classes, but also created ready-to-wear lines for the middle classes that followed the designs of haute couture but were factory made rather than custom fit to the client.

The contemporary market is essentially unchanged since the haute couture period began. There are still celebrity designers, wealthy people who have clothes that are custom made, and everyone else who wears either more expensive ready-to-wear clothes or less costly mass-market clothes. What has changed is that there is less difference in design between the high-end and the low, a reflection of the overall democratization of culture. Styles change faster than ever before, a reflection of how the modern age, with instant mass communications, demands novelty.

WHERE YOU WILL WORK

ALMOST A THIRD OF ALL FASHION designers work for clothing manufacturers, creating designs that are marketed under the brand names of their employers. While the designers themselves may be known and acknowledged among their peers in the industry, they are not among the designers known to consumers. These anonymous designers are generally referred to as in-house designers, and they generally work in studios and workshops provided by the manufacturers.

A designer working for a manufacturer, whether anonymous or someone for whom a brand has been named, often leaves the studio to go out on the manufacturing floor to oversee that designs are being made correctly. In addition, designers can appear in showrooms and at fashion shows, where they adjust and alter the clothes that are to be displayed by models.

Working at fashion shows may involve national and even international travel. Fashion designers may also travel to meet with fabric and other material's suppliers.

A third of all fashion designers are self-employed. This group is largely made up of designers who do custom work for a select clientele, and those who own their shops, or sell their clothes to small retail outlets. These fashion designers can work at home in their own studio spaces or in workrooms in the back of their shops. Designers creating fashion accessories generally require less space than designing clothing, so it is easier for them to work in a home studio.

A small number of fashion designers work in the performing arts, designing costumes for theater and dance performances. These designers may work in a college or university, or they may be on the staff of a regional theater or performing company. Very often they are independent contractors who are commissioned to create the designs for a particular show, whether at a regional theater or on Broadway. These designers also work on film and TV productions of all kinds, from independent films to Hollywood blockbusters.

The majority of fashion designers work in large cities, where there are major retail outlets, specialty stores, and the headquarters of clothing manufacturers. It is estimated that almost 75 percent of all salaried fashion designers work in New York and California.

THE WORK YOU WILL DO

FASHION DESIGNERS ENVISION clothing, accessories, and footwear, and follow their visions through to fruition. Beginning with their imaginations, they translate ideas into images that others can see, through sketches or computer graphics programs. They select fabrics, colors, and patterns. They either make the apparel themselves or direct others in the process of turning their original ideas into reality.

In some instances, the source of the inspiration will come from clients who suggest ideas of what they want. This can be a clothing manufacturer or a retailer, where the research department or marketing team has discerned a need or trend in the marketplace. It may come from a sports team wanting a new look for its players' uniforms. You might be working for a theater where the director of a play has a concept that lays out parameters for you to work within. You may get a request from an individual who needs something new and wonderful for a special occasion, such as a wedding or a ball.

Fashion designers work in a number of different areas. You may specialize in designing clothing for men or women or children. The clothing may be casual, including sportswear, or formal wear. Specialties can include outerwear, maternity, intimate apparel, or bridal gowns. Fashion designers may focus on footwear, including shoes and boots; or accessories, such as handbags, suitcases, belts, scarves, hats, hosiery, and even eyewear.

The first part of the job is understanding as much as possible about requests from clients or an employer. You may receive a clear detailed assignment, or you may need to use all your interpretive skills to determine what it is they want, and be able to demonstrate your understanding by coming up with one or more initial drawings or computer images to share.

If you are working for a particular client, the artistic side of your work will be put on hold in order to deal with business issues. The client's or employer's budget, and what the project will cost need to be determined and agreed upon. Even if it is your own company, you will still need to work up a budget to see what the project will cost you, and what you need to earn from sales. Time lines for production are a part of this phase, and identifying what individuals and other companies, such as fabric suppliers, will be required.

If you are a designer or assistant designer working on staff for an apparel manufacturer or retailer, or a freelance designer working on a contract basis, management may handle these business decisions. You may be asked for your input but final authority will rest with the business team.

The work of the fashion designer begins even before a specific project is placed on the table and even before there is an idea to be turned into a design and an actual item of clothing. It starts with the ongoing work of living your life with eyes wide open. Every street you walk down may have some image, some color, a pattern, shape or form that can provide a sudden, unanticipated inspiration. The work then involves storing these images away. You may have a vivid memory or you may have a smart phone that allows you to snap pictures every time you are struck by one of these images.

Related to this work is the more purposeful feeding of your imagination that comes from studying past and current fashion trends, both in the US and Canada, as well as from countries and cultures all around the world. You may want to keep a diary of the thoughts inspired by your research and your daily intake of images.

Among your stored images some will be more promising than others, demanding that you begin to work with them. You may begin sketching, perhaps aiming to share your early thoughts with trusted confidants or with the client for whom you are working. Sometimes you may be creating a new line without having been engaged by any specific client. In this case you will want to identify an overall theme for the collection.

The initial sketching can go through several drafts before you feel confident that you have achieved the look you are aiming for. This is where the drawing classes you took in high school, art school or college pay off, providing you with the technical skill of being able to create accurate sketches.

Your next step may be to create graphic digital images of your designs, using computer-aided design (CAD) software that will allow for additional manipulation of the design as it moves toward its definitive expression. With CAD software, designers can see virtual versions of what their work will look like when actually constructed. The software can be used to manipulate the design with adjustments to shapes and colors that would otherwise have to be done with actual fabrics.

As the design moves closer to completion, having looked at several virtual variations, the designer begins to make choices about fabric, buttons, and other elements that will be part of the realized garment. This process can involve visits to fabric manufacturers, showrooms or trade shows. It can often be a team effort, but the designer oversees the design process through to the creation of a prototype. This is shown to management or the client, toward reaching a final agreement on a specific garment, or the line of related apparel.

You may be among the team members who present new design ideas to fashion editors or fashion show management in order to predict how the market will react. Of course, if you are preparing the line for your own business then you are the one with final approval.
As a freelance fashion designer you can develop designs for a

portfolio and market your ideas to a manufacturer or retailer well before moving to the actual creation of a prototype. This is often the step taken in order to land a position with an employer, but it can be done to sell your designs while remaining independent.

From the time a design concept is first presented, to its actual production can take at least six months. With some marketers, you will work toward two delivery periods a year – one for a spring collection showing, and the other for the launch of a fall collection. That twice a year tradition is followed by many industry participants, but there are some who churn out several new collections a year in addition to the two main launches, depending in part upon the type of apparel, shoes, or accessories they sell.

As an independent fashion designer, you have an advantage over previous generations in all the electronic means of communicating with potential clients, including setting up a website and a Facebook account for your business. There are also marketplace websites such as etsy.com, where millions of individual shoppers seek out bargains in many categories, including fashion, accessories, shoes, etc. As an independent designer you can reach a wider audience than if you merely depended on foot traffic walking into your brick and mortar location. What is required is that you set up an online site that shows off your creations to best advantage and also makes interaction between you and customers as smooth as possible.
If you are not web savvy yourself, then you must find a good web designer to create the kind of site you would want to shop on yourself. Similarly, if you are going to have a retail location in addition to a web presence, you need to find someone who can build a space that fits your specifications and again demonstrates your designs to their maximum advantage.

FASHION DESIGNERS TALK ABOUT THEIR CAREERS

"I Have Worked With Several Companies as a Designer or Design Assistant

"My longest held position was as the head designer for an accessories company designing two in-house brands as well as private label for many national and international department stores.

Presently I run a sustainable graphic T-shirt line and have just finished authoring a textbook on *Textiles for Fashion*. Before I became a designer, I was working as a freelance illustrator and was trying to find work in an art-related industry where I could have regular hours and know I had a paycheck coming on a regular basis. I had always had a strong interest in fashion design. I went back to school to earn a degree in fashion design.

Working in fashion requires drive, commitment and grace. Drive will keep you working long after others have given up. Commitment will enable someone with average talent to be more successful those with less dedication to succeed. Grace in the face of adversity will always leave a good impression on others. Personal relationships can make or break you in this industry.

There is potential for great personal as well as financial reward in a fashion design career. In my own experience it has come from designing a product that so fit the required criteria from the client he called it phenomenal. Seeing my work on TV, in magazines, and out on the street is just great!

There are a good number of challenges, too. Dealing with buyers can be strenuous. Large corporations tend to want a lot for very little. It can be hard working a great design down to fit a reduced budget without losing the integrity of the original design.

I think there will be even more opportunities for new designers in the coming years. I believe the heightened awareness of good design is here to stay. With big box stores making good designs available to the masses, shows about fashion on cable TV, and style bloggers, fashion has hit the tipping point where demand is going to explode. The Internet is the key factor, opening up great opportunities for smaller fashion brands to become well known. In addition, many more stores are seeing good designs drive up their sales. This will lead to more opportunities for designers to get hired in rewarding jobs.

The best thing you can do to get started is get a sewing machine. Learn how to sew. Research fashion through periodicals and the Internet. Do costuming for the school play. Take basic art courses – fashion is an art and you need a solid foundation.

Go to the best fashion school you can get into and afford. Apply for the best internships you can find. Pay attention and work really, really hard. Fashion school is not for the weak or lazy. If this is not exactly what you want to do, don't bother. The competition is tough and you need to be ready to be driven and committed."

I Specialize in Making Wedding Dresses as Well as Dresses for the Bridesmaids in the Party

"I wasn't sure what I was going to do when I finished high school. I didn't want to go to an office every day, and I was interested in any type of career where I would be more than a secretary or file clerk, or something like that. I always loved sewing and fixing clothes, but I had not thought about it as something to do as a job, much less a career. Then the guidance counselor suggested I apply to FIT (Fashion Institute of Technology). I looked at their website and brochures, and got on the subway and went into the city to look at the school. I realized it was just where I belonged.

Many of the other students were thinking about themselves as the next Chanel or Dior, but I never felt that I had that kind of talent. What I could do was duplicate any piece of clothing I saw in a drawing or a photo. One of my girlfriends was getting married and couldn't afford the wedding dress she saw in a bride magazine and asked if I could copy it. I did and everyone loved it, and loved that I charged a fraction of what the real thing cost. Jobs started rolling in while I was still in school. Then people started asking if I could combine features from a few different dresses they liked – take the top from one and the bottom of another, change the length of the sleeve, add a bow in the back and so on. I would sketch what they asked for and when they said 'yes,' I'd make the dress for them. I could charge more for these modified dresses, too.

The work is very time consuming and while I'm well paid for each dress I make, I couldn't make as much money as a full-time job would pay. It would have been great to turn it into a business where other people carried out my design ideas, but it was always so personal to work with my clients on each detail, changes, and fittings, that I really could not figure out how to supervise anyone else doing it. Therefore, I got a regular job – which fortunately I like – working as a receptionist and general assistant in a doctor's office. The dressmaking became a supplement to my salary. Even though I have to work hard at it nights and weekends, it is great as a second income and paid for my kids to go to college, and kept the family going when my husband was laid off for a stretch from his job as an electrician.

I think if you want to be a designer, you should have an open mind about what that means. No one from my class became the next Dior, but almost everyone went on to work in the industry with good careers as design assistants, and even as full-fledged designers. Being able to say you graduated from FIT opens many doors. If this is something you want to be involved in, be ready for hard work and be prepared to follow whatever leads come your way."

I Wanted to Be an Actor but Instead Became a Costume Designer and Started Doing My Own Fashion Design on the Side

"I was in a lot of plays in high I Wanted to Be an Actor but Instead Became a Costume Designer and Started Doing My Own Fashion school and thought I was going to become a famous actress. When I got to college I didn't get cast very often because, frankly, there were a lot of people better than me. I loved the theater so much I didn't want to do anything else so I worked backstage just to stay involved. I built scenery and props, and then one day was assigned to the costume crew and that's how it started. I made costumes that some of the teachers and graduate students designed, and helped actors get in and out of them between scenes.

I took the undergraduate costume class and designed my first show when I was a junior. I discovered I had a talent for drawing I didn't know about before, and a good eye for color. Looking back, I realized that when I was little and putting on shows for my parents, I had always put together costumes and that was as much fun as my performances. So I became a costume designer, went to graduate school, got an MFA (Master of Fine Arts degree), and began to work in regional theaters around the country.

I landed a job at a university and now teach costuming, as well as designing for shows at the school and for shows at theaters around the region. Every so often, I am hired for an off-Broadway type show in a nearby city. One of the actors I worked with asked me to make her an outfit for a Halloween party, and since then I occasionally make costumes for other people as well as some fancier dress clothes and casual clothes, too.

I do not advertise or seek out this kind of work, so it is more or less a word of mouth type of thing. I'm still waiting for a boutique to ask me to design for them. Sometimes I think I should pursue it but I am very busy as it is. I think if I had a sabbatical or maybe wasn't hired for any theater work, I'd make an effort to promote my fashion work for retail stores. It might be more lucrative but also more risky and I'm not sure I want to deal with the uncertainty. There are many people in fashion who are not afraid to take risks, and I wish I could be more like that but I'm not. I think if you go into design you have to decide right from the start how much you are willing to live with risk and uncertainty. When you are starting out you're usually full of confidence and don't come to that question until it's sort of forced on you."

I Own My Own Boutique Where I Sell My Own Designs as Well as Those of People Whose Work I Admire, and Vintage Clothes, Too

"I was a stay-at-home mom with two small boys but really wanted to have a business of my own. I knew what it was going to be – a boutique where I could sell clothes I'd designed, as well as vintage clothes, and clothes of other local designers that I thought I would like to wear. The idea had been with me since I was a young girl shopping in antiques stores and vintage clothes stores with my mom who, I guess you could say was pretty much a hippy. She wasn't entrepreneurial so she had no interest in opening a store herself, but she applauded the idea that I was going to do it.

When my boys were old enough to go to school I went back to school myself and earned an AAS (Associate in Applied Science degree) in fashion design, which gave me good basics for running a business, as well as design skills. I already had a concept for the store emphasizing the combination of new and old together, as well as a concept for the design work I wanted to do. The key was affordability or affordable elegance, as I like to call it.

One of the most important things that I learned in school was the need for the right location. That was probably the biggest revelation, as I was so focused on the inside of the store and my design ideas that I had not thought about where it should be situated. Another important takeaway was learning about international resources for different materials. I was very focused on US suppliers, but one of my teachers turned me on to a list of European and South American fabric companies that had materials that were mind-blowing. I've been able to locate great sources that, even with shipping costs, are pretty reasonable. My customers recognize the quality and are willing, even in this economy, to pay a little bit more for the affordable elegance. Some larger retailers have discovered my shop, and I am negotiating, with the help of my husband who has a background in finance and accounting, a deal to start marketing my designs through them.

My head spins when I think of how fast this has been happening. I'm very lucky to have had great teachers, a supportive family, and a husband who has been 100 percent behind my doing this. It's not like we have not had setbacks, but on the whole we have had more luck than not. I have to say that if you have a dream you should go for it. You might have to wait until the time is right, like I did, but while you're waiting keep the flame burning."

PERSONAL QUALIFICATIONS

FASHION DESIGNERS ARE ARTISTS AND as such they must have strong imaginations, able to conceive of ideas that others have not had before. In order to come up with these fresh and new concepts, fashion designers must have great observation skills, because most ideas, while they may be processed internally and come out seeming original, are based on what we see and hear in the world around us. Fashion designers must be able to open themselves to ideas that can come from nature, industrial structures, military or sports uniforms, from a song, a car, or a food package. Everything is a potential source of inspiration, and the more open you are, the greater the chance of having a new vision.

Being able to translate an idea into a drawing is also an essential skill. Of course, senior designers may be able to get away with dictating a vision to draftsmen working for them. Beginners, however, are going to need drawing skills in order to present their ideas to employers, if they are working for a manufacturer, or to clients, if they are independent designers working for themselves.

In this sense, artistic ability is a communications skill. Designers also need to be able to speak effectively and write clearly to back up in words the images they are presenting. This can further be understood as an element of good business. Since so many fashion designers are self-employed, it is essential that you be familiar with marketing, bookkeeping, and other business concepts.

You must be ambitious, dedicated, and patient. Without the desire to succeed you will be hard pressed to compete against those who are determined to become the best of their generation. Your qualities may shine through, but it is a wise policy to open the window and make it easier for others to see them. For all of your hard work and desire, the success you seek could be slow in arriving. Patience is a virtue in all endeavors but in a tough, competitive industry like fashion it is especially important.

ATTRACTIVE FEATURES

AS WITH ANY ARTISTIC ENDEAVOR, there is nothing more fulfilling than to see your work on display. This can include seeing your designs in a showroom, being worn by a model, or on a stage being worn by actors. This is even more so, when you see your designs worn by a paying customer, especially a satisfied client who will show your work off to friends who may become your next clients.

There are other positive aspects to a career as a fashion designer, among them the opportunity it offers to work with other creative people. Whether a new member of a design house or a senior staffer, there is a tremendous amount of interaction among designers, their assistants, fabric specialists, colorists, retailers, marketing and merchandising personnel. Even people operating their own boutiques are likely to carry clothing by other designers, with the opportunity to interact with other creative people.

One of the most attractive aspects of being a fashion designer is the glamour potential. This is the fantasy, which does come true for some, of having your work discovered by a movie, TV, or music industry star, or a member of high society, or someone who is a celebrity, and as a result becoming a celebrity yourself. The chances of this happening are small, yet it is an element of American culture that makes this career attractive.

Glamour, by its very nature, incorporates the promise of fame and fortune. Even without becoming part of the jet set, you can do very well financially as a fashion designer and gain a fair measure of fame, even if you do not become a superstar.

If being independent is of value to you, then you certainly have the opportunity to make that happen as a fashion designer. You can decide to go your own way, opening a boutique or marketing your products through other boutiques. You will be able to choose who you want to work with and who you want to avoid.

UNATTRACTIVE FEATURES

FASHION DESIGN IS A HIGHLY COMPETITIVE industry. There are a limited number of positions within established design and manufacturing firms, and a great many people are trying to land a job whenever there is an opening available. Further, the openings, especially for newcomers, will likely be as an illustrator, or as an assistant to a designer, or some other starting spot. There is a tradition of people getting their foot in the door at the apprentice level and proving themselves as they work their way up the ladder.

If you are good enough and lucky enough to be selected from

among the many contenders, then you must be able to cope with the probability of high stress levels. Sometimes it will seem like one deadline coming right after another with no let up. Deadlines are not the only source of stress. Demanding clients are another challenge you are likely to have to deal with at some point.

These same challenges of demanding clients, repeated deadlines, and long hours are likely even if you are working on your own, not to mention the fact that you will still be competing for work or for customers against other designers. On your own, you will also have the added stress of having to run a business and market yourself in order to attract clients.

Another stress point is simply the need to keep having creative new ideas. You might, of course, be lucky enough to create one great design that you can live off of for years. But, as with creative people in all sorts of art and design categories, if you come up with something wonderful, the pressure will be on to do it again.

EDUCATION

YOU CAN BECOME A FASHION designer without going to college by putting together a portfolio and applying for openings with clothing manufacturers, retailers, design firms, or in a theatrical costume shop. An outstanding portfolio can land you a position in one of these venues as an intern or as an assistant designer.

Nevertheless, there are dozens of colleges and universities in the US and Canada with accredited fashion design degree programs, and there are solid benefits to be had from going to one of them. Part of the value of attending one of these schools are the connections you make with faculty members who also work in the industry, and the connection to alumni who have gone on to have success in the industry, as well as the contacts with your fellow students. Even people who did not attend the school you attend will be aware of the quality education available there and respect your being a graduate.

Beyond these networking benefits, attending a college or university with a fashion design program can make a significant difference in your career because of what you can learn about the basics of design, fabrics, and the business of fashion. You have the option of earning a two-year associate degree (AAS), a four-year bachelor's (BA), or Bachelor of Fine Arts (BFA) degree. In addition, several schools offer a Master of Fine Arts degree (MFA), which will be very helpful if you want to have the opportunity to teach or become involved in the very important work done at museums on costume preservation and restoration.

AAS Degree

An Associate of Applied Science degree in fashion design is offered at many colleges and technical schools. The application process for such a degree usually includes submitting a sample of your creative work. At the Parsons The New School For Design, for example, applicants are asked to submit "a collage that defines the lifestyle of the kind of woman or man for whom you would like to design." The application information recommends that applicants "use images taken from magazines and pay attention to colors, textures, and other basic elements."

Among the courses in the Parsons AAS degree program are:
Color Theory
Construction: Draping
Construction: Pattern Making
Construction: Sewing
Design History
Fashion Digital
Fashion Drawing
Fashion Technical Drawing
Fashion Techniques

Part of the AAS coursework focuses on creating your own portfolio, a basic necessity when you begin job hunting. Having a portfolio is a requirement for entering the BFA program at Parsons. The portfolio is expected to contain eight to 12 pieces that can be "drawings, paintings, photographs, digital media, design, three-dimensional work, web design, animation, video, and other digital media."

BFA Degree

The BFA coursework at Parsons goes much further than the AAS degree in developing student design skills, focusing on the creative process involved in fashion design development, including the relationship between research and inspiration; balancing technical proficiency and aesthetic sensibility; and the "transition of 2D concepts to 3D product, through, design, pattern making and draping, and the acquisition of basic technical skills."

Students are encouraged to maintain a journal about the development of their design ideas and the evolution of their creative process. Schools offering BFAs typically have studio space where candidates can work on their individual projects or on group projects.

MFA Degree

Although MFA programs include academic classes on fashion history and aesthetics, they tend to be heavily focused on the practical development of each student's skills to a professional level under close guidance of a faculty member. At the Academy of Art University in San Francisco, for example, the MFA fashion curriculum in the Graduate School of Fashion "refines and focuses the graduate candidate's individual vision" through the extensive use of directed study in studio courses culminating in a final thesis project which is the production of a professional fashion collection and portfolio. The Academy selects the best collections for presentation at its Annual Fashion Show in San Francisco, and at shows taking place in New York City during that city's annual Fashion Week.

While most of the course work is hands-on, there are classroom requirements that focus on such subjects as art history awareness, aesthetic sensitivity, cross cultural understanding, and business-oriented courses in communications skills for fashion designers.

It is important to emphasize the value of a degree-oriented program in learning how to develop a portfolio, that collection of design samples that displays your ideas and abilities, which is critical when it comes to being hired for a design position, even as an intern or assistant. While you can figure out how to create a portfolio on your own, degree programs almost always focus on how to do it, the current presentation standards, and professional criticism of your effort in order to help you make it better.

Sources

There are several sources for identifying colleges and universities that offer fashion design courses. The National Association of Schools of Art and Design (NASAD) establishes national standards for undergraduate and graduate degrees in several areas, including fashion design. A list of its over 300 members can be found on its website.

The website Fashionista offers an excellent guide to the top 20 schools in the US.

The Toronto Fashion Incubator (TFI) is a great source for all kinds of information about the Canadian fashion industry. This nonprofit organization, which is dedicated to supporting and nurturing small business entrepreneurs, includes a listing on its website of 35 Canadian fashion schools.

EARNINGS

THE MEDIAN ANNUAL EARNINGS FOR fashion designers are about $65,000, meaning half of those working in the US make less than that and half make more. The lowest 10 percent in this field earn about $35,000, while the top 10 percent earn in excess of $130,000.

It is common for starting salaries for designers to be very low and increase according to tenure and the reputation they build for themselves. On average, designers who join management will receive the highest salaries, while those who design for performing arts groups, sports teams, and in other areas of the entertainment field tend to make the lowest salaries. This is only about averages, however, and the spread in income from one costume designer to another can be very great.

In general, fashion designers working for an employer usually earn higher incomes than self-employed designers who may have their own boutiques or work on a contract basis for other employers. The incomes of full-time employees are more stable, as well. They also usually receive benefits, including health insurance, paid vacations, and retirement and pension contributions.

Of course, this is a career that holds out the promise of great wealth, far above the average earnings. There is a definite fantasy element that affects artists in many categories, which is to achieve widespread recognition and with it fame and fortune. There are a number of renowned fashion designers, usually heading their worldwide manufacturing and marketing firms, who make millions. In addition to making their own apparel lines, these designers earn large sums from licensing their name and brands to endorse all sorts of products, in addition to clothing.

OUTLOOK

GROWTH IN THE NUMBER OF FASHION designers employed will be only moderate in coming decades. Mainstream apparel manufacturers are not expected to increase hiring substantially. There will be competition for new jobs from students graduating from fashion design programs. Although new opportunities will be limited overall, there will be spots open in specialized design niches, for example, athletic clothing using newly developed fabrics.

Self-employed fashion designers will increase in number. This may be understood as a result of an ever-expanding desire for independence among young fashion designers. The economy is in recovery and people are always looking for bargains, hoping to find the best quality and value they can. As an independent fashion designer, you can find ways to serve the needs of your immediate community, and from that starting point look to expand into a broader client base through word of mouth and self-promotion.

GETTING STARTED

PUTTING TOGETHER A FIRST RATE portfolio can be considered the most important thing to do on your path to becoming a professional fashion designer. If you are enrolled in a college or university fashion design program, a focus of your studies will be on how to create a portfolio. Some technical schools will also help you learn how to prepare a winning portfolio.

If you are not pursuing a degree program and not at a technical school that offers training in portfolio preparation, there are still ways to get help in putting one together. The Internet has many websites that show portfolios from students at leading fashion schools as well as the portfolios of freelance fashion designers. The website www.styleportfolios.com not only features the portfolios and résumés of up-and-coming designers, but also offers details on creating your own portfolio. Click on portfolio/create a portfolio for specific help in getting started.

There is a good job board for fashion designers at www.stylecareers.com

If you are going on to a university, then you will almost certainly have networking opportunities as faculty members in many of the fashion design departments are working professionals as well as teachers. Of course, all of your classmates will be seeking their support and endorsement just as you are. The extent to which you are given support could be an indicator of what your strengths and weaknesses are and what you need to do in order to advance into a professional career.

If you are not in a school where you have access to professionals who can help you network, you should consider what other contacts you have made through your interning and volunteer work. If you have not done either of those, then you should begin, not only for the actual experience it provides but also for the networking opportunities.

Any leads you get, whether through networking or in your initial job hunting, must be followed up swiftly and intently. Never forget how competitive the market is for fashion designers and do not hesitate to take any work that will get you in the door, whether as an intern, an assistant, doing cutting or sewing, or dressing models or actors.

Continue to improve your knowledge of color and fabric as well as your skills such as drawing. Continue to observe and seek inspiration in the world around you. Be open, think boldly, and do not give up!

ORGANIZATIONS

- **American Apparel & Footwear Association**
www.wewear.org
- **Association of Sewing and Design Professionals**
www.paccprofessionals.org
- **California Fashion Association**
www.calfashion.org
- **Canadian Apparel Federation**
www.apparel.ca
- **Costume Society of America**
www.costumesocietyamerica.com
- **Council of Fashion Designers of America**
http://cfda.com
- **Council of International Fashion Designers**
www.miamifashionweek.com/Council_of
_International_Fashion_Designers.html
- **Fashion Business Incorporated**
http://fashionbizinc.org
- **The Fashion Center**
www.fashioncenter.com

■ **Fashion Design Council of Canada**

www.lorealfashionweek.ca

■ **Fashion Footwear Association of New York**

http://ffany.org

■ **Fashion Group International**

www.fgi.org

■ **National Association of Schools of Art and Design**

http://nasad.arts-accredit.org

■ **Fashionista**
http://fashionista.com/2011/07/the-top-20-fashion
-schools-in-the-united-states-the-fashionista-ranking

■ **National Association of Sustainable Fashion Designers**
www.sustainabledesigners.org

■ **Surface Design Association**
www.surfacedesign.org

■ **Toronto Fashion Incubator**
www.fashionincubator.com

■ **Young Fashion Designers' Association**
www.fashionindustrynetwork.com/forum/topics
/the-young-fashion-designers-3

PERIODICALS

- Allure
- Complex
- Cosmopolitan
- Elle
- Fashion
- Flaunt
- Glamour
- Harper's Bazaar
- InStyle
- L'Officiel
- Lucky
- Marie Claire
- MAO
- Nifty
- Nylon
- Seventeen
- Teen Vogue
- V
- Vogue
- W

SCHOOLS

■ **Academy of Art University**

http://www.academyart.edu

■ **Fashion Institute of Technology**

http://www.fitnyc.edu

■ **Parsons The New School For Design**

http://www.newschool.edu/parsons